OCEAN TRENCHES AND DEEP-SEA LIFE

Lisa Perlman Greathouse

Consultants

Dr. Aaron O'Dea, Dr. Erin Dillon, Dr. Natasha Hinojosa, and Dr. Kimberly García-Méndez
Researchers
Smithsonian Tropical Research Institute

Cheryl Lane, M.Ed.
Seventh Grade Science Teacher
Chino Valley Unified School District

Michelle Wertman, M.S.Ed.
Literacy Specialist
New York City Public Schools

Publishing Credits

Rachelle Cracchiolo, M.S.Ed., *Publisher*
Emily R. Smith, M.A.Ed., *SVP of Content Development*
Véronique Bos, *VP of Creative*
Dani Neiley, *Editor*
Fabiola Sepulveda, *Art Director*

Smithsonian Enterprises

Avery Naughton, *Licensing Coordinator*
Paige Towler, *Editorial Lead*
Jill Corcoran, *Senior Director, Licensed Publishing*
Brigid Ferraro, *Vice President of New Business and Licensing*
Carol LeBlanc, *President*

Image Credits: p.10 AIP Emilio Segrè Visual Archives, Gift of Bill Woodward, USNS Kane Collection; p.11 [LC-2010586277]; p.12 Alamy Stock photo/ODI; p.13 National Oceanic and Atmospheric Administration Science Source; p.14 (top) NH 96801 U.S. Navy Bathyscaphe Trieste (1958–1963), Art collection, U.S. Naval History and Heritage Command website. Released by the U.S. Navy Electronics Laboratory, San Diego, California; p.14 (bottom) NOAA Ship Collection/Archival Photography by Steve Nicklas, NOS, NGS; pp.17–21, 32 NOAA Office of Ocean Exploration and Research; p.21 (bottom) Alamy Stock photo/Mark Conlin; p.23 (left) NOAA/Image courtesy of John McCord UNC CSI – Battle of the Atlantic expedition; p.23 (right) Bridgeman Images/Prismatic Pictures; p.24 Wiki/Francis Godolphin Osbourne Stuart; p.25 (top) Getty Images/Ralph White; p.25 (bottom) Newscom/National Geographic/Album/Newscom; p.26 NOAA Office of Ocean Exploration and Research; all other images from Shutterstock and/or iStock

Library of Congress Cataloging-in-Publication Data
Names: Greathouse, Lisa E., author. | Smithsonian Institution.
Title: Ocean trenches and deep-sea life / Lisa Perlman Greathouse.
Description: Huntington Beach, CA : Teacher Created Materials, Inc., 2025. | Series: Earth & space science | "Smithsonian"--Cover. | Audience: Ages 10-20 | Summary: "Earth's oceans are vast and mysterious. Scientists have learned about the lowest parts of our planet by studying deep ocean trenches. The seafloor is not a flat, static place. It has earthquakes, volcanoes, and a variety of unique species!"-- Provided by publisher.
Identifiers: LCCN 2024039557 (print) | LCCN 2024039558 (ebook) | ISBN 9798765968918 (paperback) | ISBN 9798765968994 (ebook)
Subjects: LCSH: Submarine trenches--Juvenile literature. | Deep sea biology--Juvenile literature.
Classification: LCC GC87.6 .G74 2025 (print) | LCC GC87.6 (ebook) | DDC 577.7/9--dc23/eng/20240902
LC record available at https://lccn.loc.gov/2024039557
LC ebook record available at https://lccn.loc.gov/202

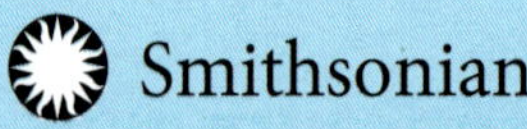

5482 Argosy Avenue
Huntington Beach, CA 92649
www.tcmpub.com
ISBN 979-8-7659-6891-8

Printed by: 51497
Printed in: China

Table of Contents

What Lies Beneath the Surface?

For centuries, people have wondered what lurks below the surface of Earth's oceans. Beneath the glistening water, oceans are complex, mysterious, **dynamic**, and deep. And because Earth's surface is about 70 percent water, that means most of the surface of our planet is under the oceans. Movies and books have explored the subject, sometimes playing off our fears of the unknown. What strange creatures might lurk deep in the darkness below?

Scientists have been studying the very bottom of Earth's oceans for decades. They have discovered the ocean floor holds answers to questions about our planet's formation. Scientists once thought the ocean floor was a flat, still, and boring place. Now, we know the seafloor is always changing. Frequent earthquakes and volcanic eruptions can shake things up. And creatures unlike anything on Earth's surface live in the depths. The deep sea is the largest **biome** on Earth.

Think of the ocean floor the same way you think about land on Earth. There are multiple levels: flat plains, gentle hills, towering mountain peaks, and deep **trenches**. There's a lot to learn about the world under the water's surface, so let's dive in!

FUN FACT

This 1972 photo of Earth from outer space is called *The Blue Marble*. In the image, you can see how much water makes up the planet's surface.

Oceanic Structure

If you're seeking the deepest valley on Earth, you won't find it on land. It's deep in the ocean! The deepest ocean trench reaches roughly 10,935 meters (35,876 feet) below the water's surface. The way ocean trenches form is tied to the structure of Earth's crust. The crust is a thin layer of rock that makes up Earth's surface. Continental crust exists on land, and **oceanic crust** exists at the bottom of oceans.

All of Earth's land—both above and below water—sits on tectonic plates. These are like huge puzzle pieces of Earth's crust. They are made of solid rock. Under each plate is a weaker layer of partially melted rock. For hundreds of millions of years, these plates have been shifting around and bumping into each other. As the plates move, the continents on them move, too. The theory of plate tectonics explains how plates move and interact with one another.

The structure of the oceans is caused by the way tectonic plates move over time. The shallowest parts of oceans are along the edges of continents. They are called *continental shelves*. They are extensions of what's found on the land around them. For example, shelves along the coastline of plains are flat or gently sloping. Shelves along mountainous coasts are steep. Shelves **descend** toward the deep ocean floor in what is called the *continental slope.*

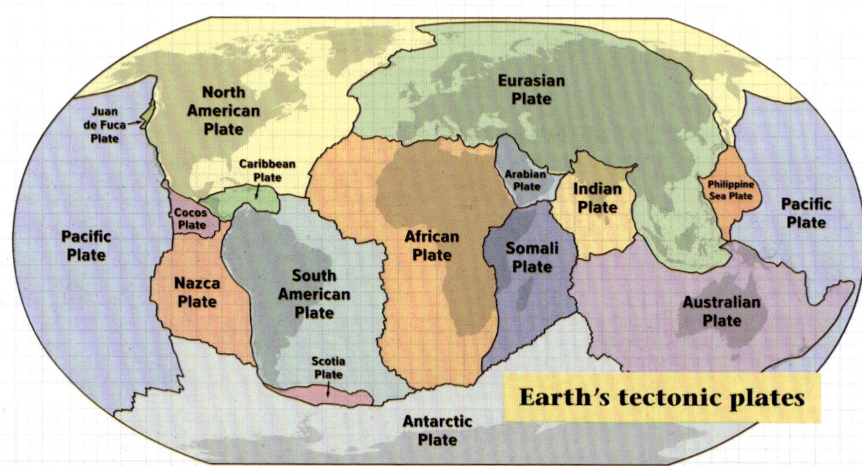

Earth's tectonic plates

Ocean Depths

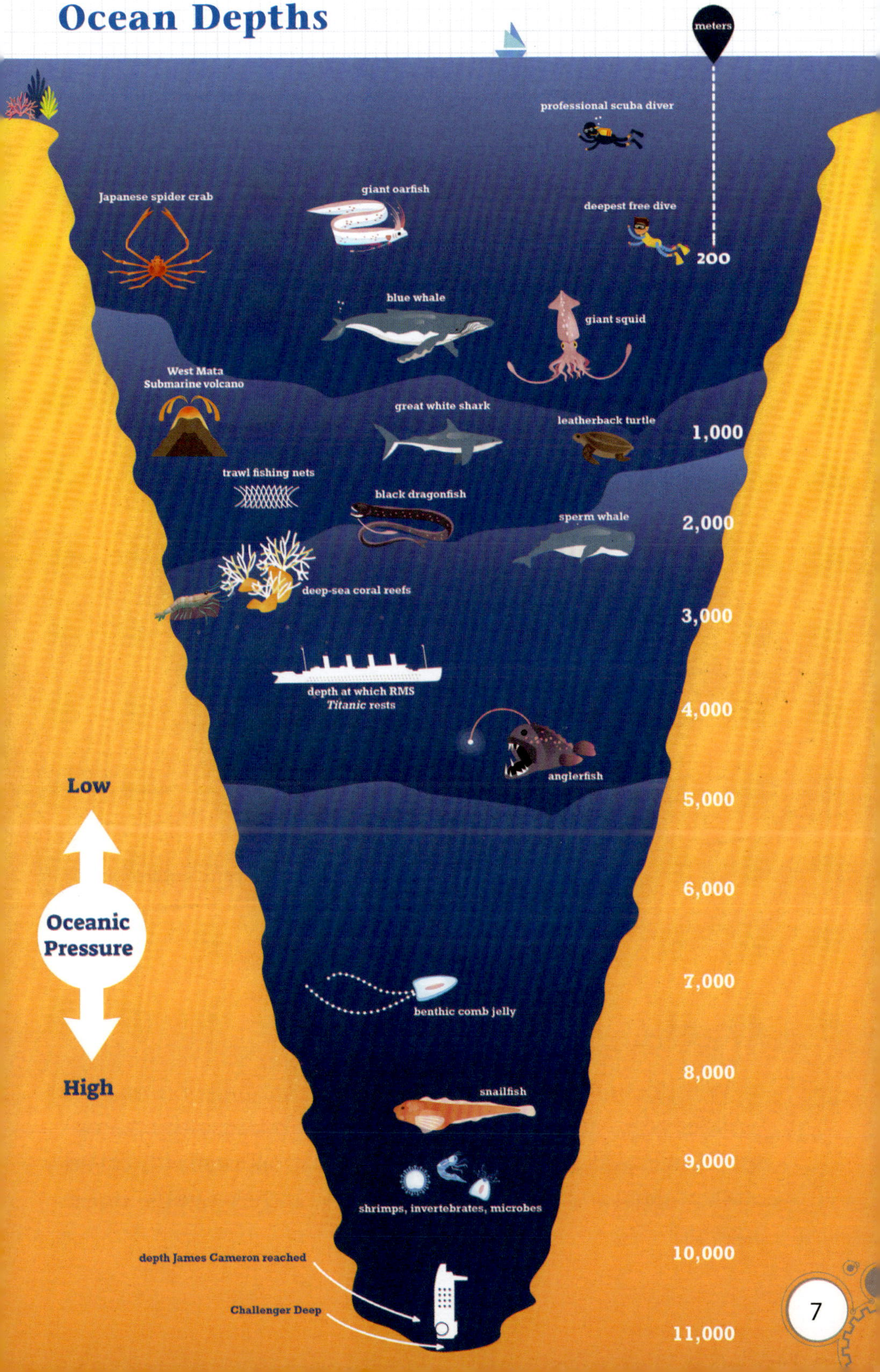

meters

professional scuba diver

Japanese spider crab

giant oarfish

deepest free dive

200

blue whale

giant squid

West Mata Submarine volcano

great white shark

leatherback turtle

1,000

trawl fishing nets

black dragonfish

sperm whale

2,000

deep-sea coral reefs

3,000

depth at which RMS *Titanic* rests

4,000

anglerfish

Low

5,000

Oceanic Pressure

6,000

7,000

benthic comb jelly

High

8,000

snailfish

9,000

shrimps, invertebrates, microbes

depth James Cameron reached

10,000

Challenger Deep

11,000

Plate Movement

The collisions of tectonic plates can cause earthquakes and volcanic eruptions, both on land and in the water. Underwater earthquakes can sometimes result in tsunamis. These are giant walls of water. When they crash ashore, they can cause widespread destruction.

Sometimes, when the edges of tectonic plates rise up, underwater mountain ranges are formed. Other times, one plate may slide under another plate. Areas where this occurs are **subduction** zones. When two plates meet at a subduction zone, a deep ocean trench can form.

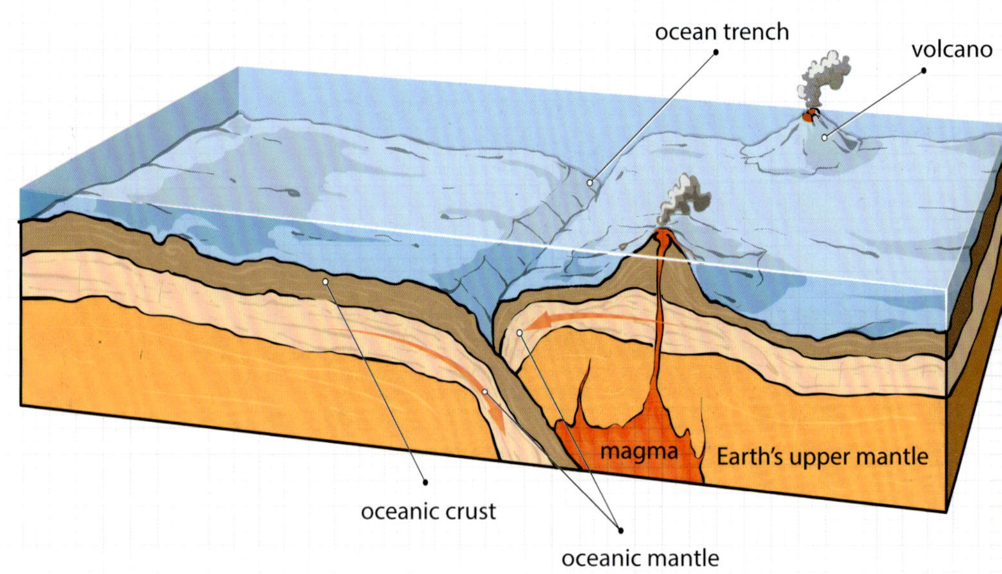

Seafloor Spreading

With tectonic plates sliding under each other, you might wonder why Earth isn't shrinking. That's because the plates sometimes pull apart instead. When that happens, it's called *seafloor spreading*. It may only be a few inches a year—but it adds up!

Seafloor spreading creates a new seafloor. You might expect valleys or trenches to form where plates pull apart. But instead, **magma** fills in the gaps. When seafloor spreading happens slowly, it can result in steep cliffs and mountains on the ocean floor. When it happens quickly, it can cause gentle slopes and result in new geographic features. For example, the Red Sea was created when the African plate and the Arabian plate split apart.

Seafloor spreading occurs when magma rises up to the boundaries of two tectonic plates.

SCIENCE

Ring of Fire

Deep trenches can be found in all oceans, but most are found in the Ring of Fire. This is a ring-like area around the Pacific Ocean. Its name comes from its many volcanoes and earthquakes—and fire-hot lava! Nearly 90 percent of all earthquakes occur along this ring.

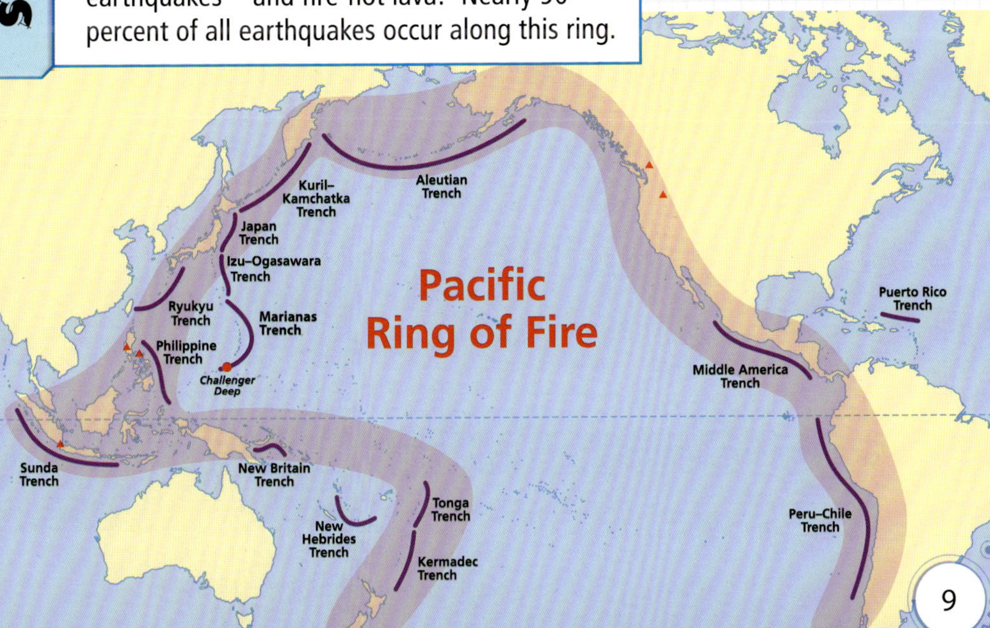

Discovering the Mid-Atlantic Ridge

Plate tectonics explains how Earth's surface is broken into larger pieces of crust that move. This theory gave **geologists** a way to understand how Earth's surface has evolved. Before scientists discovered plate tectonics, they assumed the seafloor was flat and unchanging. However, they couldn't have been more wrong.

In the 1950s, scientists began learning more about the ocean floor. A **cartographer** named Marie Tharp began mapping the ocean floor. She worked with her colleague, Bruce Heezen. Heezen went onto research **vessels** to collect data. These vessels collected **sonar** data. Then, Tharp examined the data and plotted it onto a map. Her findings surprised many researchers. Instead of a plain, flat environment, Tharp had charted something very different. The landscape she mapped was complex. Just like on land, there were steep mountains, deep trenches, and sprawling plains.

One of the pair's most incredible finds was the Mid-Atlantic Ridge. This huge underwater mountain range spans the entire length of the Atlantic Ocean! In some parts, it is up to 1,500 kilometers (932 miles) wide. It is the longest mountain range on Earth. It follows a curving path from the Arctic Ocean to the southern tip of Africa. Some of the mountains in this range go above the surface of the ocean to form islands. Iceland is one of the islands formed by this mountain range.

Marty Weiss, Al Ballard, and Marie Tharp work on the research ship USNS *Kane* in 1968.

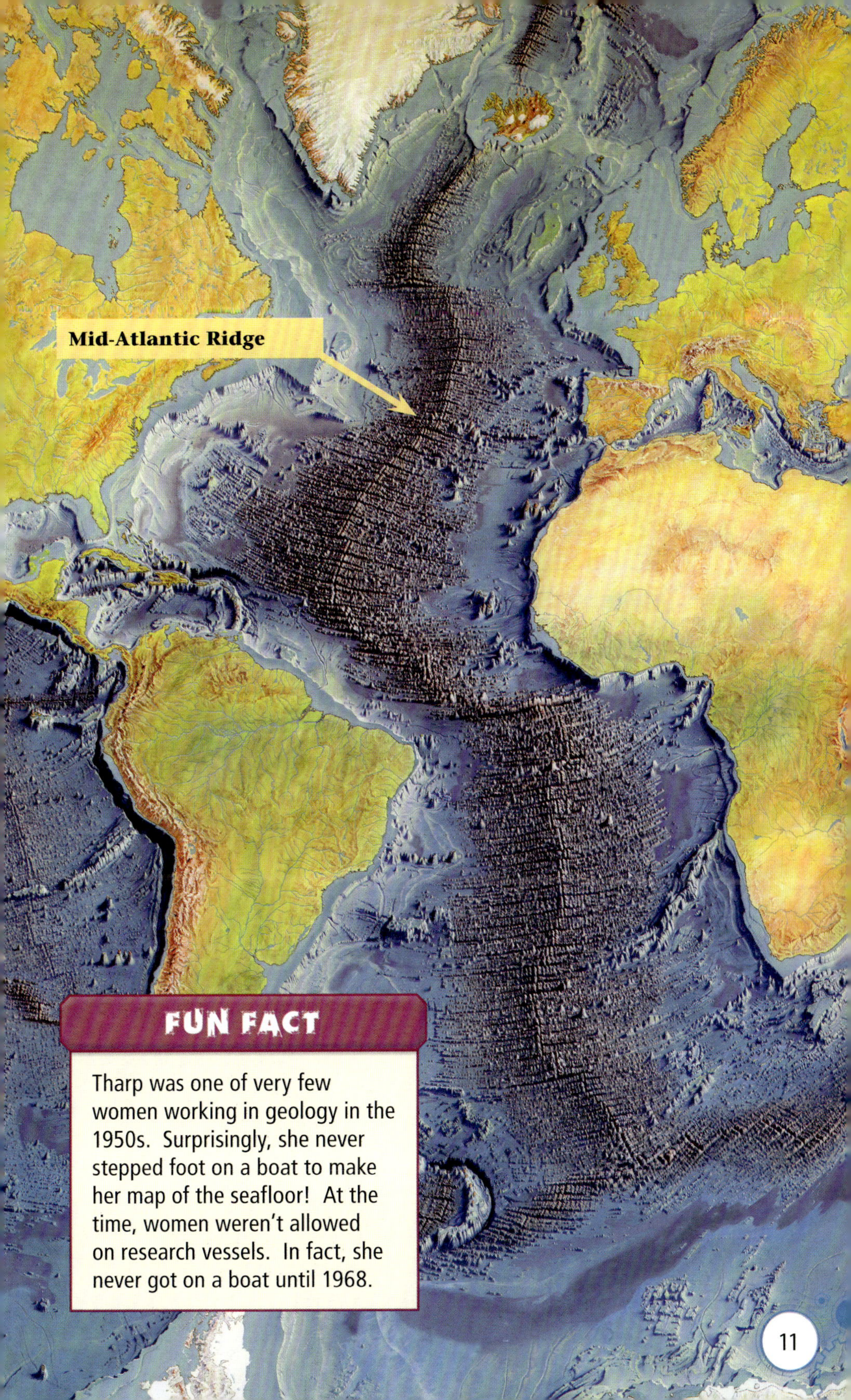

FUN FACT

Tharp was one of very few women working in geology in the 1950s. Surprisingly, she never stepped foot on a boat to make her map of the seafloor! At the time, women weren't allowed on research vessels. In fact, she never got on a boat until 1968.

Evidence of a Rift Valley

At the time of Tharp's work, the idea of plate tectonics was controversial. So, when Tharp found evidence of a huge valley within the Mid-Atlantic Ridge, she was surprised. Her calculations pointed to evidence of a rift valley. This is a low-lying place on Earth that forms when Earth's tectonic plates rift, or move apart. Tharp kept rechecking her calculations. If there was indeed a valley, that would mean the mountains she was mapping included a place where the oceanic crust was spreading apart. It would support the idea of seafloor spreading *and* plate tectonics. But at first, no one believed what Tharp had found—not even Heezen! It took months for her to convince him. Once it became clear that this rift went through the entire ocean, Heezen and other scientists believed her.

Today, some scientists refer to the Mid-Atlantic Ridge as a spreading center. It is a place where the tectonic plates pull apart slowly, about 2 to 5 centimeters (0.8 to 2 inches) per year. The tallest parts of the ridge are connected by a deep rift valley between them. The valley is up to 3 km (2 mi.) deep. That is about the depth and width of the Grand Canyon! In this valley, magma comes to the surface of the ridge through Earth's crust. It is cooled by the deep ocean water and is pushed away, forming new crust.

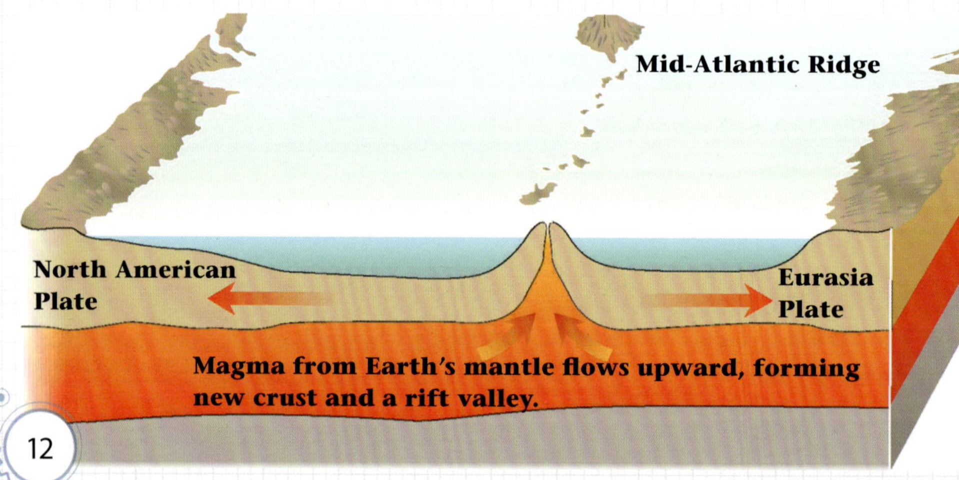

Magma from Earth's mantle flows upward, forming new crust and a rift valley.

The West Mata volcano erupts 1,219 m (4,000 ft.) below the surface of the Pacific Ocean.

TECHNOLOGY

Sonar

Sonar uses sound waves to detect the location and size of underwater objects. First, sound waves are sent out into the water. When the waves hit an object, reflections, or echoes, return to a receiver. These reflections tell where and how far away an object is.

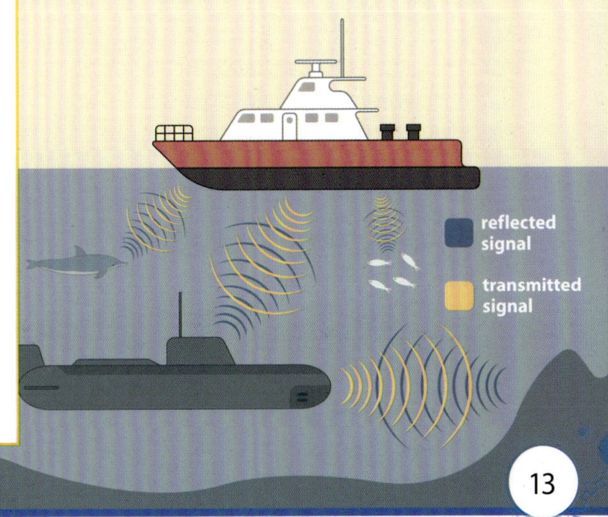

Challenger Deep

It's hard to fully grasp just how vast and deep Earth's oceans are. Over 70 percent of the planet is covered by the Atlantic, Pacific, Indian, Arctic, and Southern Oceans. The average depth of our oceans is about 3,600 m (11,811 ft.). But, there are spots that are much deeper—in fact, more than three times as deep.

The deepest known point of our oceans is the Challenger Deep. It is part of the Mariana Trench in the Pacific Ocean, near the island of Guam. It is 10,935 m (35,876 ft.) deep. That is almost 11 km (7 mi.). It is so deep that you could fit Mount Everest inside. That is Earth's highest point on land. And still, Everest's peak would be more than a mile below the surface of the water! The Mariana Trench is long, too. It stretches for about 2,550 km (1,580 mi.) underwater.

The Mariana Trench formed from the movement of tectonic plates. Long ago, two plates collided. One plate was forced under the other. The old oceanic crust slid downward, creating a deep trench.

ENGINEERING

Exploring the Deep

Jacques Piccard and Lieutenant Don Walsh were the first people to go to the bottom of the Mariana Trench. They used a **submersible** called the *Trieste*. On January 23, 1960, they reached a depth of around 10,916 m (35,814 ft.). The whole journey took about nine hours to complete.

Piccard and Walsh travel in the *Trieste* (above).

Farallon de Pajaros
Maug Islands
Asuncion
Agrihan
Pagan
Alamagan
Guguan
Zealandia Bank
Sarigan
Anatahan
Farallon de Medinilla
NORTHERN MARIANA ISLANDS (U.S.)
Saipan
Tinian
Aguijan
Rota
GUAM (U.S.)
Mariana Trench
Challenger Deep

Under Pressure

As of July 2022, just 27 people have traveled down to the depths of the Mariana Trench. A big reason why the deepest parts of our oceans are such a mystery is because they are not safe for humans and are difficult to access. Diving that deep means experiencing dangerous conditions. For example, underwater **vents** can spew out liquids that range from 60 °C (140 °F) to greater than 400 °C (752 °F). In other spots, the water is near freezing. Plus, there is no light. But the biggest challenge is the extreme pressure.

When diving to the bottom of a swimming pool, you may get an unpleasant feeling in your ears and sinuses. That is because the deeper you go, the more pressure there is. The weight of the water above pushes on any object below it. So, the lower a diver descends, the more water pushes down and against them. The farther down they go, the more intense the pressure. It is recommended that most advanced recreational divers only reach 40 m (130 ft.) deep. At the bottom of the Mariana Trench, the pressure can be about one thousand times the pressure at sea level!

Luckily, scientists have created other ways to explore the deepest parts of the oceans. Remotely operated vehicles, or ROVs, can survive the depths. These vehicles do not have people in them and are controlled from above the water. Specially built submersibles can also withstand the pressure. These vehicles allow scientists to take photos and measurements of the seafloor.

An ROV is brought back to the water's surface after diving deep in the Arctic Ocean.

MATHEMATICS

Dive In!

When divers jump off the side of a boat, math plays a big part in staying alive underwater. Divers prepare by studying temperatures and charts that help them calculate how many minutes they can safely dive at different depths. Due to the intense pressure, the deeper they dive, the less time they can safely stay under water. Plus, they can only carry so much air for their time underwater.

What Lives Down There?

What kinds of creatures could possibly survive the harsh conditions of the deep sea? They would have to be able to tolerate extreme heat and freezing cold. Don't forget the intense pressure and total darkness.

Believe it or not, the seafloor ecosystem is crawling with life. Scientists estimate that there are 2.2 million species in our oceans. And they have only identified a small fraction of them! Studying these species in the intense pressure of the deep sea is a difficult task. But what scientists have learned is that deep-sea species are unlike species in shallow waters. And those differences can tell us a lot about how the environment shapes life underwater.

Deep-sea species tend to have unusual appearances. There are hairy snails and ghostly shrimp. There are tiny octopuses and "zombie worms" that burrow into whale bones to eat the fat inside. Some of these organisms are **translucent**, so you can see their insides. This protects them from being spotted by predators in the darkness. A commonly found species is **xenophyophores**, which look like they would grow on a coral reef. Scientists have discovered small sea cucumbers and **amphipods**, which are little underwater scavengers.

ghost fish in the Mariana Trench

Snails attached to hot water vents were found at a depth of 980 m (3,215 ft.).

This jellyfish was found at 3,700 m (12,139 ft.).

deep-sea cucumber

This blind lobster was found at 675 m (2,215 ft.).

Unusual Creatures Abound

Scientists discovered a new deep-sea species of octopus. They nicknamed the species the "flapjack octopus" because their bodies make them look like pancakes. Their bodies bounce when they swim, and they have webbing between their arms. Their fins are on their heads, and they help with swimming. This species is so cute that scientists considered giving it the scientific name *adorabilis*—a play on the word *adorable.*

A flapjack octopus can grow up to 50 centimeters (20 inches) in size.

tripod fish

The tripod fish gets its name from its long fins. It pumps fluid into its fins to make them look like stilts or a tripod. It rests on its fins and waits for prey to come by. Meanwhile, its top fins can detect predators swimming above it. Since this fish has very small eyes, it relies on its fins to sense the environment around it.

The Mariana snailfish is believed to hold the record for the deepest living fish on the seafloor. One was found at 7,966 m (26,135 ft.) deep! This species looks a bit like a tadpole. It has a bulging head and a partly transparent body. It has winglike fins that help it hunt for food, and it is thought to be one of the top predators along parts of the Mariana Trench.

The aptly named fangtooth fish has large, sharp teeth. This species only grows to about 15 cm (6 in.) long, but it can eat much larger fish because of its big jaw and large teeth. It has limited eyesight and finds its prey by sensing movement.

fangtooth fish

Inspiration of the Deep

Humans have always been intrigued by the mysteries of the oceans. But, it's not just researchers who have looked to the sea for inspiration—so have all types of artists. For centuries, images of the deep sea have been represented in our culture and art. Some of the first modern **atlases** included artwork of scary sea creatures. Earth's oceans have inspired some of our most famous literature, music, film, art, poetry, and music. The oceans are also well represented in the Bible and in Greek mythology. As long as humans have been on Earth, the deep sea has been a great source for stories.

Some artists join research vessels and go on **voyages** to the ocean floor. Along the way, they see firsthand some of the creatures of the deep bathed in the vehicles' lights. Then, when they resurface, they paint these creatures so other people can truly appreciate the beauty of what lies below. Some artists have even used real **sediment** from the ocean floor in their artwork.

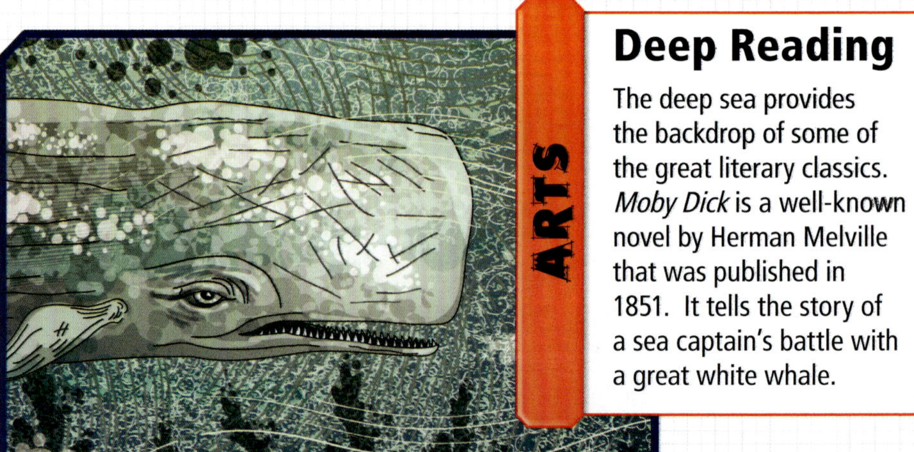

ARTS

Deep Reading

The deep sea provides the backdrop of some of the great literary classics. *Moby Dick* is a well-known novel by Herman Melville that was published in 1851. It tells the story of a sea captain's battle with a great white whale.

Scientists prepare for a dive in a submersible.

illustrations of deep-sea life from 1923

Exploring a Shipwreck

The true story of the RMS *Titanic* has inspired art and intrigue about the bottom of the sea. On April 14, 1912, this luxury passenger ship was on its first voyage. As it traveled from England to New York, it hit an iceberg and sank to the bottom of the Atlantic Ocean. More than 1,500 people lost their lives. Hundreds of people escaped on lifeboats.

Immediately, people wanted to bring the ship to the surface. But they couldn't figure out how to withstand the immense pressure of the seafloor. Plus, they didn't know the exact location or condition of the ship. For decades afterward, the exact site of the wreckage remained a mystery. In 1985, it was found at last. A marine geologist named Dr. Robert Ballard and an **oceanographer** named Jean-Louis Michel worked with a team of explorers. They found the wreckage at a depth of about 3,800 m (12,500 ft.). It was near the coast of Newfoundland, Canada. In 1986, a submarine and an ROV were used to explore the wreckage. Today, scientists around the world continue to study the *Titanic*.

RMS *Titanic*

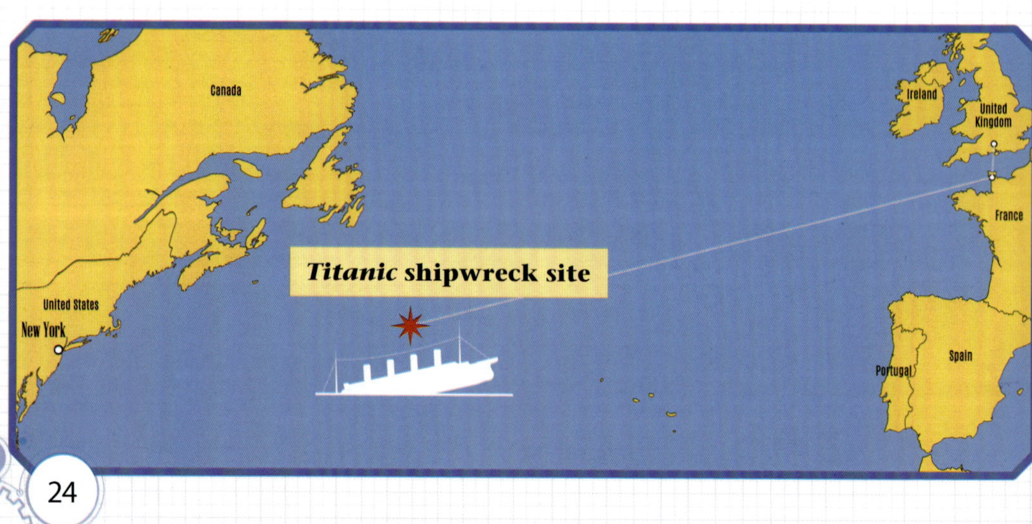

***Titanic* shipwreck site**

A spare anchor can be seen on the deck of the shipwrecked *Titanic.*

Since then, thousands of artifacts have been recovered from the ship. The story of the *Titanic* has inspired many works of art, including poems, songs, paintings, and films.

The 1997 hit movie *Titanic* was based on the disaster and the search for the wreckage. The director, James Cameron, made more than 30 dives to the wreckage site. His real-life search for the *Titanic* inspired him to make the film.

FUN FACT

James Cameron is among the people who have traveled to the bottom of the Mariana Trench. He made the journey by himself in a special capsule. He discovered new species, including a sea cucumber and squid worm!

Mysteries of the Deep Remain

Earth's oceans have unique structures and are full of fascinating creatures. Scientists have only explored about five percent of our oceans. The intense pressure, coldness, and darkness of deep water make the oceans difficult to explore. Ocean trenches, the deepest parts of our planet, contain many unsolved mysteries.

Still, scientists do all they can to learn about these remote places on Earth. Scientists think ocean trenches could hold many answers to questions about how Earth functions. Trenches have shown us how the movement of tectonic plates causes continents to move over time. Deep water shows us how species can adapt to harsh conditions.

An ROV takes pictures of an underwater vent for scientists to study.

The ribbon sawtail fish is found at depths over 500 m (1,640 ft.).

In the past few decades, scientists have made huge advances in deep-sea exploration. What they have learned so far hints at the existence of previously unknown species and ecosystems. They also hint at how nature is affected by humans. The more we learn, the more we believe these remote areas may play a vital role in our lives on land. They may also provide insight into earthquakes and volcanoes. But until we find ways around the challenges of exploring the deepest points of the sea, more questions will remain than answers. As always, scientists continue to collect data on our underwater world, bringing light to the darkness.

STEAM CHALLENGE

Define the Problem

Near the Ring of Fire, nearly 20 different ocean trenches exist. This means that for people living in the area, earthquakes and tsunamis are a constant threat. Architects are seeking new construction ideas for buildings that can withstand earthquakes and tsunamis. To help the architects, you will design and test a structure model against both catastrophic events.

Constraints: You may only use the materials provided to you.

Criteria: Your structure must fit onto a paper plate and must be at least 46 centimeters (18 inches) tall. It must remain standing without structural damage during both the mock earthquake and tsunami.

Research and Brainstorm

How do earthquakes affect human-made structures? What are the current designs that architects are using? In what way do tsunamis damage structures? How can one design withstand both natural disasters?

Design and Build

Using your research, sketch a model of your structure. Be sure to label the materials you will need and how it will be fastened to your paper plate. Meet with your team members to discuss each of your ideas. Then, create one final design using the best ideas from all participants. Collect the materials needed and build your model.

Test and Improve

Two group members will place the model on a desk at the front of the room. Holding onto opposite sides of the plate, the group members will push and pull the plate for 15 seconds to simulate an earthquake. Then, they will place the plate into a bin filled with water and put a weight on top of the plate. Two group members will hold the sides of the bin, sloshing the water back and forth gently for 15 seconds to simulate a tsunami. After this, remove the model and inspect it for damage. What modifications can you make? Make adjustments and retest.

Reflect and Share

What surprised you during this challenge? What hardships did you and your team have to work through? How may different building materials play a part in how earthquakes and tsunamis affect them?

Glossary

amphipods—group of small crustaceans, or animals that have exoskeletons and two pairs of antennae

atlases—books of maps

biome—a major type of ecological community (such as a tropical rainforest)

cartographer—a person who makes maps

descend—to move downward

dynamic—characterized by constant change

geologists—scientists who study the history of Earth and its life, especially as recorded in rocks

magma—molten rock material within Earth

oceanic crust—the thin part of Earth's crust that is beneath the oceans

oceanographer—a scientist who studies the oceans

sediment—solid material (such as stones and sand) deposited by water, wind, or glaciers

sonar—a method for detecting objects underwater by sending out sound waves that are reflected back

subduction—process in plate tectonics when the edge of one tectonic plate slides under another

submersible—a small underwater craft used for deep-sea research

translucent—not transparent but clear enough to allow light to pass through

trenches—long, narrow depressions or ditches in the ground

vents—openings for the escape of gas or liquid, or for the relief of pressure

vessels—ships or boats

voyages—long journeys

xenophyophores—single-celled organisms that live at depths of 500 to 10,600 m (1,640 to 34,777 ft.) in the oceans

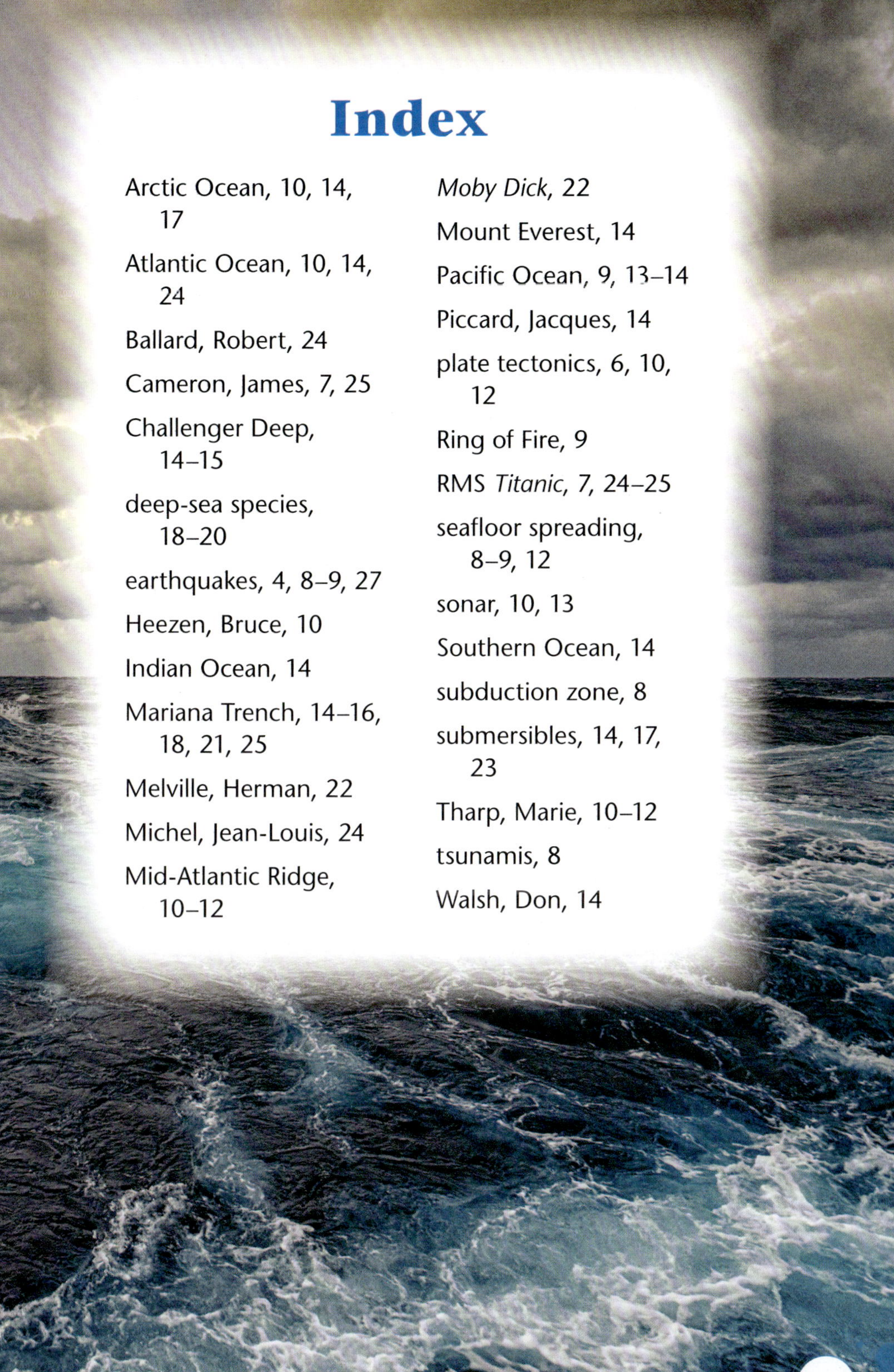

Index

from Smithsonian

Do you want to study the oceans?

Here are some tips to keep in mind for the future.

"Build a model of an ocean trench using clay or sand. It's a fun way to visualize the incredible depths of our oceans."

– *Dr. Erin Dillon, Postdoctoral Researcher, Smithsonian Tropical Research Institute*

"Examining maps of the ocean floor is an amazing way to explore our planet's underwater landscapes and ocean trenches."

– *Dr. Kimberly García-Méndez, Lab Manager, Smithsonian Tropical Research Institute*

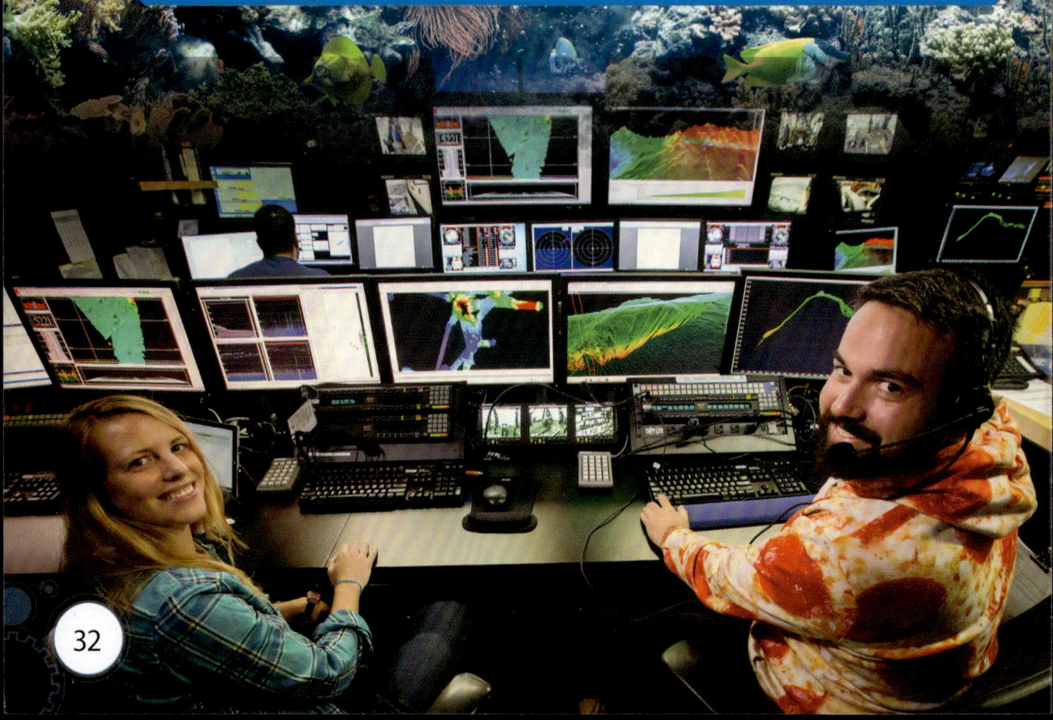